Your Government:
How It Works

The Internal
Revenue Service

JoAnn A. Grote

Arthur M. Schlesinger, jr.
Senior Consulting Editor

Chelsea House Publishers
Philadelphia

CHELSEA HOUSE PUBLISHERS
Production Manager Pamela Loos
Art Director Sara Davis
Director of Photography Judy L. Hasday
Managing Editor James D. Gallagher
Senior Production Editor J. Christopher Higgins

Staff for THE INTERNAL REVENUE SERVICE
Project Editor/Publishing Coordinator Jim McAvoy
Associate Art Director Takeshi Takahashi
Series Designers Takeshi Takahashi, Keith Trego
Editorial Assistant Rob Quinn

The Chelsea House World Wide Web address is
http://www.chelseahouse.com

First Printing
1 3 5 7 9 8 6 4 2

Library of Congress Cataloging-in-Publication Data

Grote, JoAnn A.
    The Internal Revenue Service / JoAnn A. Grote.
        p. cm. — (Your government — how it works)
    Includes bibliographical references and index.
    ISBN 0-7910-5989-8
    1. United States. Internal Revenue Service—History—Juve-
nile literature. 2. Income tax—United States—History—Juvenile
literature. [1. United States. Internal Revenue Service. 2. Taxation—History.] I. Title. II. Series.

HJ2361 .G76 2000
336.24'0973—dc21   00-034577

Contents

YOUR GOVERNMENT HOW IT WORKS

Introduction

Government: Crises of Confidence

Arthur M. Schlesinger, jr.

FROM THE START, Americans have regarded their government with a mixture of reliance and mistrust. The men who founded the republic understood the importance of government. "If men were angels," observed the 51st Federalist Paper, "no government would be necessary." But men are not angels. Because human beings are subject to wicked as well as to noble impulses, government was deemed essential to assure freedom and order.

The American revolutionaries, however, also knew that government could become a source of injury and oppression. The men who gathered in Philadelphia in 1787 to write the Constitution therefore had two purposes in mind: They wanted to establish a strong central authority and to limit that central authority's capacity to abuse its power.

To prevent the abuse of power, the Founding Fathers wrote two basic principles into the Constitution. The principle of federalism divided power between the state governments and the central authority. The principle of the separation of powers subdivided the central authority itself into three branches—the executive, the legislative, and the judiciary—so that "each may be a check on the other."

YOUR GOVERNMENT: HOW IT WORKS examines some of the major parts of that central authority, the federal government. It explains how various officials, agencies, and departments operate and explores the political organizations that have grown up to serve the needs of government.

Introduction

The federal government as presented in the Constitution was more an idealistic construct than a practical administrative structure. It was barely functional when it came into being.

This was especially true of the executive branch. The Constitution did not describe the executive branch in any detail. After vesting executive power in the president, it assumed the existence of "executive departments" without specifying what these departments should be. Congress began defining their functions in 1789 by creating the Departments of State, Treasury, and War.

President Washington, assisted by Secretary of the Treasury Alexander Hamilton, equipped the infant republic with a working administrative structure. Congress also continued that process by creating more executive departments as they were needed.

Throughout the 19th century, the number of federal government workers increased at a consistently faster rate than did the population. Increasing concerns about the politicization of public service led to efforts—bitterly opposed by politicians—to reform it in the latter part of the century.

The 20th century saw considerable expansion of the federal establishment. More importantly, it saw growing impatience with bureaucracy in society as a whole.

The Great Depression during the 1930s confronted the nation with its greatest crisis since the Civil War. Under Franklin Roosevelt, the New Deal reshaped the federal government, assigning it a variety of new responsibilities and greatly expanding its regulatory functions. By 1940, the number of federal workers passed the 1 million mark.

Critics complained of big government and bureaucracy. Business owners resented federal regulation. Conservatives worried about the impact of paternalistic government on self-reliance, on community responsibility, and on economic and personal freedom.

When the United States entered World War II in 1941, government agencies focused their energies on supporting the war effort. By the end of World War II, federal civilian employment had risen to 3.8 million. With peace, the federal establishment declined to around 2 million in 1950. Then growth resumed, reaching 2.8 million by the 1980s.

A large part of this growth was the result of the national government assuming new functions such as: affirmative action in civil rights, environmental protection, and safety and health in the workplace.

Some critics became convinced that the national government was a steadily growing behemoth swallowing up the liberties of the people. The 1980s brought new intensity to the debate about government growth. Foes of Washington bureaucrats preferred local government, feeling it more responsive to popular needs.

But local government is characteristically the government of the locally powerful. Historically, the locally powerless have often won their human and constitutional rights by appealing to the national government. The national government has defended racial justice against local bigotry, upheld the Bill of Rights against local vigilantism, and protected natural resources from local greed. It has civilized industry and secured the rights of labor organizations. Had the states' rights creed prevailed, perhaps slavery would still exist in the United States.

Americans are still of two minds. When pollsters ask large, spacious questions—Do you think government has become too involved in your lives? Do you think government should stop regulating business?—a sizable majority opposes big government. But when asked specific questions about the practical work of government—Do you favor Social Security? Unemployment compensation? Medicare? Health and safety standards in factories? Environmental protection?—a sizable majority approves of intervention.

We do not like bureaucracy, but we cannot live without it. We need its genius for organizing the intricate details of our daily lives. Without bureaucracy, modern society would collapse. It would be impossible to run any of the large public and private organizations we depend on without bureaucracy's division of labor and hierarchy of authority. The challenge is to keep these necessary structures of our civilization flexible, efficient, and capable of innovation.

More than 200 years after the drafting of the Constitution, Americans still rely on government but also mistrust it. These attitudes continue to serve us well. What we mistrust, we are more likely to monitor. And government needs our constant attention if it is to avoid inefficiency, incompetence, and arbitrariness. Without our informed participation, it cannot serve us individually or help us as a people to attain the lofty goals of the Founding Fathers.

American colonists grew so angry with paying unfair taxes that they would tar and feather tax collectors.

CHAPTER 1

Fighting Against Taxes

"NOTHING IN LIFE IS certain but death and taxes."

Have you ever heard that popular saying by Benjamin Franklin? Death is certain. Most people believe some **taxes** are certain. But income taxes are not certain.

Income taxes are such a part of our lives today that we sometimes forget our citizens haven't always paid income taxes. In fact, the Constitution originally did not allow income taxes.

Income tax is just what it sounds like, a tax on income, or the money people and companies make. It is only one kind of tax. Other kinds of taxes include sales taxes on things people buy, property taxes on things people own, and **tariffs**, which are taxes on things brought into the country and sent out of the country.

Although Americans haven't always paid income taxes, they've almost always paid taxes of some kind. And it seems they've always been rebelling against taxation.

Americans have been rebelling against unfair taxes since we were only British colonies and not a country. Colonists weren't against all taxes. They knew governments needed money. American colonists were against taxes they considered illegal or unfair.

Some of the earliest **tax rebellions** led to the Revolutionary War. The **Stamp Tax** of 1765 caused the first major tax revolt. The British government passed the Stamp Tax. People in America had to pay the tax.

Under the Stamp Act, people had to pay taxes on each business piece of paper. It was called the Stamp Act because the papers were stamped to show the tax had been paid. Everything made of paper was taxed—newspapers, marriage certificates, college diplomas, and even decks of cards.

Patrick Henry became a lawmaker in Virginia shortly after the Stamp Act was passed. He and some other lawmakers were angry about the tax. They reminded their fellow lawmakers that the colonies had always made their own tax laws. Britain had taxed things it sold to the colonies before. But Britain had never made a law like the Stamp Act, which taxed things that people in the colonies sold to other colonists.

Patrick Henry also reminded the Virginia lawmakers that there were no lawmakers from the American colonies in the British Parliament. He said that meant the people in the colonies were being taxed without representation. Taxation without representation was against British law, so the Stamp Act was illegal. Patrick Henry argued that American colonists should only have to obey laws made by colonial lawmakers.

Soon Americans in all the colonies were crying, "No taxation without representation!" Many decided not to buy anything from Britain until the Stamp Act was repealed, meaning it would no longer be a law. Many lawyers

Patrick Henry stated that there should be no taxation without representation, when a British tax was placed on all items made of paper in the colonies.

stopped going to court. They didn't want to pay taxes on their legal papers and have them stamped.

Men in many cities and towns formed a secret club called the Sons of Liberty. They put up posters warning people not to sell Britain's tax stamps or use them. In some places people were so angry they covered tax collectors with sticky tar and feathers and chased them out of town.

Many merchants in Britain were upset over the Stamp Act, too. They were losing money because people in America were not buying their goods. They wanted the lawmakers in Britain to repeal the Stamp Act. So the British lawmakers did.

The colonists were still paying other taxes. Under the Sugar Act of 1764 they paid taxes on sugar, molasses, coffee, wine, and indigo. In 1767 the Townshend Acts were passed in another attempt to raise money from the colonies. This law taxed glass, lead, paint, paper, and tea shipped to the colonies. (These taxes are also called **duties.**)

Again many colonists agreed not to use British goods until British lawmakers repealed the Townshend Acts. Some of America's future Revolutionary War heroes joined in the protest.

George Washington ordered his agent in London to send him nothing that was taxed by Britain. "I have very heartily entered into an association not to import any article which now is, or hereafter shall be, taxed for this purpose until the said act or acts are repealed," he wrote.

Attacks on tax collectors, who were also called customs officers, grew worse. The most serious attacks took place in Boston. Britain's king sent soldiers to Boston to protect the tax collectors so the taxes could be collected. Ben Franklin warned the king's advisors that the Bostonians wouldn't like being forced by soldiers to pay the taxes they felt were unfair.

Ben Franklin was right. In March 1770 there was an argument between the soldiers and some Boston citizens. Soldiers fired their guns. Five citizens were killed and six wounded. The deadly argument became known as the Boston Massacre.

The next month, the British lawmakers repealed all the taxes under the Townshend Act except the tax on tea. They did not think the colonists would mind paying this one small tax. They could not have been more wrong.

Colonists objected loudly to the tax on tea. Tea was one of the main drinks of adults and children in the colonies, but many colonists stopped drinking it. Not everyone quit drinking it. Some started drinking smuggled tea instead. Smuggled tea was illegal.

Tea grown in Britain's other colonies was to be sent by boat to Britain and sold to British merchants. Then the British merchants sold the tea to people in America. That made the tea more expensive to the Americans. To get around this, people began smuggling tea into America. So much tea was smuggled that the British tea merchants lost a lot of money.

Britain sent armed ships to stop the smuggling ships. The British ships were called **revenue** ships, because their purpose was to enforce the revenue and tax laws. In 1772 colonists attacked and burned a revenue ship called the *Gaspee* off Rhode Island. A large reward was offered by Britain for information on the attackers. Most colonists wanted tea smuggling to continue, so they did

In Boston in 1770 a group of British soldiers fired into a crowd of angry colonists. The soldiers were enforcing the Townshend Acts, which had created new taxes.

not give Britain enough evidence to bring the attackers to trial.

Samuel Adams, one of our Founding Fathers, said, "Our greatest apprehension is that these proceedings may be preparation to new taxes; for, if our trade may be taxed, why not our lands? Why not the products of our lands and every thing that we possess or use?"

British ships filled with tea were sent to America. Most ports sent the tea ships away. In Boston the governor of Massachusetts said the ships could not leave Boston Harbor until the tea was unloaded.

In December of 1773 a group of Boston men including Paul Revere disguised themselves and boarded the ships. They opened the tea boxes and threw the tea into the harbor. The event became known as the Boston Tea Party.

When all the tea had been dumped the men marched merrily down the wharf. Where the wharf reached the land, a window in a building flew open. The British admiral stuck out his head. He'd watched everything. "You have got to pay the fiddler yet," he warned. Everyone knew the admiral meant someone would have to pay for the tea, or people would be punished.

He was right. In May 1774 a ship from Britain brought news of the king's punishment. Beginning the first day of June, Boston would be closed to all boats and ships. It would stay closed until the people of Boston paid for the tea. The king also sent soldiers to Boston to make sure no ships were allowed to enter or leave Boston harbor except British warships.

Americans in all the colonies were furious, but none were as angry as those in Boston. Bostonians never paid for the tea. Tensions grew between British soldiers and Americans. Finally in 1775, in a little town called Lexington near Boston, British soldiers and Americans fired guns at each other. The American Revolution had begun.

THE DESTRUCTION OF TEA AT BOSTON HARBOR.

The Americans soon found it wasn't easy to raise enough money to pay for a war. The people who suffered most were probably the Continental soldiers, the standing army of America at that time. At first, people thought that local fighting forces, the militias (citizen-soldiers) would be the core of the war effort. They feared that a permanent army would later be a danger to freedom in America. So they did not want to help out the Continental army with money and supplies. One of the places the soldiers suffered most was at Valley Forge with General George Washington.

Boston's colonists protested taxes by throwing a shipment of tea into the harbor. Following the Boston Tea Party, tensions grew, and the Revolutionary War began.

General George Washington and his troops struggled during a winter spent in Valley Forge, due to a lack of funds and supplies. The Continental Congress was not allowed to create taxes, and America had to borrow money from other countries and private citizens to support the war effort.

CHAPTER 2

Life Without Taxes

VALLEY FORGE, PENNSYLVANIA, IS where General George Washington and the American army stayed during the winter of 1777 and 1778. Much of the British army stayed in Philadelphia, only about 20 miles away.

Valley Forge wasn't a city like Philadelphia. Valley Forge was only a place in the country along the Schuylkill River. There weren't houses to stay in, or bakeries, or stores like there were in Philadelphia.

General Washington's men had to build their own houses. They cut down trees and built 700 wooden huts without windows. Until the huts were built, the men lived in tents.

General Lafayette described what he saw at Valley Forge. "The unfortunate soldiers were in want of everything; they had neither coats, nor hats, nor shirts, nor shoes; their feet and legs froze till they grew black, and it was often necessary to amputate them. . . . The army frequently passed whole days without food."

General Lafayette's tour of the Continental army's camp at Valley Forge led him to press the French government to support the American Revolution. Although the military and financial aid the French sent to the United States were welcomed, they also left the former colonies with enormous debt.

General Washington wrote, "Our difficulties and distresses are certainly great, and such as wound the feelings of humanity. Our sick naked, and well naked, our unfortunate men in captivity naked!" Another time he wrote of seeing " . . . men without clothes to cover their nakedness, without blankets to lie on, without shoes (for the want of which their marches might be traced by the blood from their feet)."

The Continental Congress had as much trouble keeping men armed with weapons, called arms, as they did

keeping the soldiers fed and clothed. Baron von Steuben, a Prussian general who helped train the soldiers, tells us in his writings, "The arms at Valley Forge were in a horrible condition, covered with rust, half of them without bayonets, many from which a single shot could not be fired."

At the beginning of the winter, General Washington had about 10,000 soldiers at Valley Forge. As the season continued, about 2,500 men left the army. Some went home or joined the British, with whom they could be warm and have clothes and food.

About 2,500 died from starvation, cold, and sickness. They died from starvation because they did not have enough to eat. They died from the cold because they did not have enough clothes and blankets. And they died from sickness because the army did not have enough medicine. There were many reasons the army did not have these things. All the reasons had to do with money.

The Congress during the Revolutionary War was called the Continental Congress. The Continental Congress did not have the right to make tax laws to raise money. When

The freezing conditions and lack of supplies at Valley Forge took a great toll on the Continental army. During the course of the winter, what had begun as an army of close to 10,000 men dwindled to nearly half that number as sickness and low morale soon left Washington's forces in shambles.

Only states could tax their people when our country was first created. So members of the Continental Congress created their own currency, called Continentals, to help fund the Revolution.

the army needed money, General Washington would ask Congress for it. The only way Congress could get the funds was to ask the states. If the states decided to give Congress money, the states would tax their own people for it.

Often the states would give Congress only a little of the money Congress asked them to send. Many Americans thought it was foolish to pay taxes to the state when they were fighting a war over having to pay taxes to Britain.

Some people did not mind paying taxes to help the American soldiers who were from their own states. They did not think they should have to pay for food, clothes, and weapons for soldiers from other states.

Congress printed money called Continentals. They printed so much money that it was not worth anything. General Washington said toward the end of the war that a wagon loaded with Continentals would only buy no more than a wagon filled with supplies for the army. By 1781 a pound of tea cost 90 Continental dollars. When a person thought something was not worth anything he would say "It's not worth a Continental."

Congress borrowed money from other countries such as France and Spain, but one day that money would have to be paid back.

After the war Congress had many bills, or **debts,** to pay. It owed money to Americans who had loaned Congress money for the war, to other countries who had helped America, to Americans who had supplied items to the army, and it owed money to the soldiers for fighting in the army and navy. In all, Congress owed $8 million to other countries and $32 million to Americans for the war.

But Congress had no way to raise the money.

In arming the colonists against England, America soon owed a large debt to other countries. Once the war was over, Congress had a problem: it owed millions of dollars in loans but had no way to repay its debts.

CHAPTER 3

To Tax or Not to Tax

THE NEW AMERICAN STATES struggled in the years after the war. Money was always a problem. The amount of money they owed grew. The Continental Congress kept asking the states for money, but the states did not give Congress very much. The states needed money to run their own governments.

After a few years the American leaders decided they needed stronger laws. In 1787 they wrote a new constitution. One of the most important issues was how to raise money. People remembered British leaders using the power to tax unfairly. They did not want Americans to ever pay more than their fair share of taxes to help pay the country's bills.

Finally, the leaders agreed to let Congress make tax laws. But they told Congress which kinds of taxes they could collect. They also told Congress what reasons it must have to collect taxes. These rules were

Early America struggled without money. In order to make collecting taxes easier, it was written into the Constitution that Congress could create laws which would tax the entire country to pay for debts, defense, and the welfare of the people.

written into the country's new Constitution of the United States of America.

It took the states years to agree on the new Constitution. In 1790 the last state agreed to it, and it became law.

This is what the Constitution said about taxes: Congress could demand taxes to pay the country's debts, to defend the country, and "for the general welfare" of the country. "The general welfare" meant the money had to be used for things important to all the people in the country, not only for people in one place. The taxes also had to be "equally apportioned." That meant they had to be the same everywhere in the country. Congress could not tax some people but not all people. It could not tax some people more than other people.

The first tax law Congress passed was the Tariff Act. An act is another name for a law. A tariff is a tax on things brought into the country **(imports)** or sent out of the country **(exports)** to be sold.

Congress created the Department of the Treasury to be in charge of all money matters. Now that Congress had a law to raise money, it needed people to collect the money. The Customs Service was started to do this. It was called **customs** because the taxes it was to collect were customs, or tariff, taxes. The Department of the Treasury was put in charge of the Customs Service.

Things were better for the country after the Tariff Act was passed. The money collected on imports and exports helped pay the country's many bills. But it wasn't enough money.

So in 1791 Congress passed the first **internal tax.** This wasn't a tax on things that were sold to other countries or brought into the United States from other countries, like a tariff tax (an external tax). This was a tax on something made in the United States and sold in the United States. The tax was called the Whiskey Tax. It taxed alcoholic drinks and things made from tobacco.

The commissioner of the revenue was given the job of collecting the taxes. He couldn't do it alone. Tax assessors and tax collectors were hired. Tax assessors went to places where whiskey and tobacco products were made. They decided how much tax was owed. The taxes were paid to the tax collectors. Their pay depended on how much tax they collected. Records were kept of who owed which taxes and when and how much they paid. The money was sent to the United States Treasury.

People who made and sold whiskey did not like this tax. They thought it was unfair. Why should they be taxed when other people who made and sold things in the United States weren't taxed? Didn't the Constitution say everyone had to be taxed alike?

Some people who made whiskey in Pennsylvania refused to pay the tax. In 1794, tax collector John Neville and a U.S. marshal went to tell the whiskey makers that

The Whiskey Rebellion in Pennsylvania in 1794 started when the government created a tax on alcohol and tobacco. Refusing to pay the new tax, a group of people assaulted tax collectors sent to retrieve the money.

they had been ordered to go to court. They were to tell why they would not pay their taxes. The whiskey makers were so mad that they fired guns at Neville and the marshal, who managed to get away without being hurt.

The next morning the angry men surrounded Neville's home. They carried guns and clubs. They wanted him to quit his job. Neville said no. People fired guns, and Neville fired back. Neville wasn't hurt, but he killed 5 men.

The next day, 500 angry people returned to Neville's home. Again they demanded Neville quit his job, and again Neville said no. This time the people burned Neville's home and stole his possessions. President Washington was angry that people would harm someone who was only doing his government job. He ordered soldiers to Pennsylvania to stop the uprising.

On November 13, 1794, people suspected of being involved in the raid on Neville's home were arrested. People who thought the whiskey makers were right to rebel called this "the Dismal Night." The rebels were brought to trial. Only two were found guilty. They were sentenced to be hanged, but President Washington pardoned them.

The Whiskey Rebellion, as it was called, was an important event in our country's history. It proved the new government thought the tax laws were important and would use force to make people follow the laws.

Congress passed more internal tax laws. Among other things, they taxed carriages and sugar. People did not like all these internal taxes. But they remembered the Whiskey Rebellion and did not revolt again. Instead, they were careful about who they voted for in the elections. In the 1800 election they voted for Thomas Jefferson as their third president. Under Jefferson the Congress got rid of all the internal taxes.

It took a war for Congress to pass more internal taxes.

The U.S.S. Constitution *is seen here in a battle with the British ship the* Guerriere *during the War of 1812. Wars have always been expensive and have usually been paid for by increases in taxes.*

CHAPTER **4**

War and Taxes

THE WAR OF 1812 reminded America how expensive war is. The tariffs did not bring in enough money to pay for the war.

Once more Congress passed internal tax laws. People paid property taxes on their houses, land, and slaves. Sales taxes were paid on alcoholic drinks and things made from tobacco again, and on furniture, gold and silver watches, silverware, and jewelry.

The commissioner of the revenue hired more tax assessors and tax collectors to help collect all the new taxes. The tax collectors listed everyone from whom they collected taxes. They made many copies of the list. One copy went to the commissioner of the revenue, and one was posted at the local courthouse, where everyone could read it.

It was important for the government to raise money quickly to pay for the war. They gave tax collectors special rights so they could collect the money as fast as possible. They were allowed to enter homes and businesses to look for proof that people weren't paying their taxes.

The collectors did not need to wait for a judge to say they could go into people's homes and businesses, as other law officers had to do. If people refused to pay the taxes the collectors said they owed, the collectors could take their property to pay the tax without going to court.

In 1817, after the war was over, Congress repealed the internal tax laws. It also ended the jobs of the commissioner of revenue and all the assessors and tax collectors for internal taxes. Those who collected tariff taxes did not lose their jobs. They continued to work for the Customs Service. The special rules for tax collectors, however, weren't ended. Congress felt collecting the government's money was so important the special rules were needed.

For many years the United States government raised all its money by tariffs and sales of land. Then came another war. This time it was a long and expensive one—the Civil War. It started in 1861. The cost in both lives and money was greater than anyone expected. Soon the war was costing the Northern states alone over $1 million a day. To pay for this war Congress passed the first income tax in 1861. It was considered a tax on wealthy people because only people with over $800 a year in income were taxed. Congress forgot one important item. There was no one to collect the tax. The government only had tax collectors to collect tariffs. In 1862 Congress passed another law, which made the internal revenue system a permanent part of our government. "Internal revenue system" means a system to collect income, or revenue, from internal taxes. Internal taxes are taxes on things that are not sent out of the country or brought into the country.

President Lincoln established the Bureau of Internal Revenue. Each Union state was divided into collection districts. The districts were not established in the Southern states, which were fighting the Northern states in the Civil War. As the law ordered, a tax assessor and tax collector were hired for each district. A commissioner of internal

The Bureau of Internal Revenue, which would later change its name to the Internal Revenue Service, was created during the Civil War to help collect the ever growing list of taxes.

revenue was hired to run the new Bureau of Internal Revenue.

The bureau was not in charge of collecting only income taxes, which were **direct taxes** (paid by the people to the government). Congress had ordered other internal taxes to help pay for the war. There were taxes on alcohol and tobacco products again, on insurance companies, banks, advertisements, meat, railroads, ferryboats, perfume, cosmetics, medicine, and playing cards, among other things. These were **indirect taxes,** to be paid when goods and services were purchased. Congress decided 33 kinds of businesses would need licenses, or they would not be allowed to stay in business. The licenses were given by the Bureau of Internal Revenue.

Six months after the law was passed, almost 4,000 people worked for the Bureau of Internal Revenue. There were 366 assessors and collectors for the 183 collection districts. There were 3,456 deputy collectors and assistant assessors to help the assessors and collectors. About 60 male and female clerks worked with the commissioner in his office in Washington, D.C.

The bureau needed all these people. There was a lot of work to do. The assessors went through the districts and located everything and everyone that was supposed to be taxed. They decided when a tax was to be paid. They listed the items and people and gave the list to the district tax collector.

It was the collector's job to collect the tax. It was too much work for the collector and his assistants to go to every person and business place that owed taxes. Collectors' offices were set up in each district. The people who were to pay taxes would come to the office to pay.

Author Mark Twain paid income tax in 1864 of $36.82. He also paid a fine of $3.12 for paying the tax late. The famous writer joked that it made him feel "important" that the government was paying attention to him.

In addition to their salary the assessors were given more money for every 100 names on the lists they gave the collectors. And in addition to the tax collectors' salaries they were given part of all the money they collected. In the first year they collected $39.1 million. That only paid for 39 days of war. When the war was over, the country owed almost $3 billion.

As in every kind of business, some assessors and collectors were honest people, and some were not. Soon taxpayers were saying the assessors and collectors were collecting too much in taxes, so they could make the extra money. Four years after the Bureau of Internal Revenue was started, Congress appointed a committee to "reform" it because of these charges.

The committee decided some of the charges against the assessors and collectors were true. Congress decided that any revenue employees who cheated the government out of money or did not tell of others they knew were cheating, would pay large fines.

Congress gave the commissioner of the revenue power to appoint 25 supervisors. These supervisors were to watch for internal revenue employees who were not honest with the citizens. The commissioner could also hire detectives to help prevent people from cheating the government out of money. Soon the title of "detective" was changed to "agent."

In 1872 the income tax was repealed. Congress knew that when the income tax was discontinued, the country would need other ways to raise money. In 1868 they increased taxes on alcoholic beverages and tobacco products. From that time until 1913 almost 90 percent of internal taxes were on these products.

That meant a big change in the work of internal tax assessors and tax collectors.

Moonshine operations, where people made and sold their own alcohol, proved a problem for early tax collectors. Not only did moonshiners not want to pay their taxes, they sometimes said so by shooting at the people who came to collect them.

CHAPTER 5

Whiskey Wars

THE UNITED STATES HAS taxed alcoholic beverages and tobacco products more than any other items. In 1790 the first internal taxes were on these products. That tax resulted in the Whiskey Rebellion. Now similar taxes caused more trouble for people who made the products and the tax assessors and collectors.

Alcoholic beverages were often called "distilled spirits." The people who made them were called "distillers." One of the assessors' jobs was to determine the amount of spirits a distiller made, so the right amount of tax could be charged. The Treasury Department bought instruments to help the assessor do this. Laboratories were built where the amount of alcohol in beverages could be measured.

If a distiller did not pay the tax, the collectors were to destroy the spirits. Sometimes they destroyed the "still" where the spirits were made, so the distiller could not make more untaxed spirits. Many farmers who lived far from cities made corn into whiskey. Often their stills were difficult for revenue agents to find.

People began attacking the **revenue agents** who looked for stills and tried to collect the taxes. Many agents were killed by illegal distillers. Revenue agents began taking U.S. marshals and other law officers with them to protect them from angry distillers.

The revenue agents shut down many illegal distilleries and tobacco operations. When agents shut down such places in North Carolina, the residents became angry. Local judges issued warrants against the agents saying the agents had broken North Carolina laws. Then Congress made a law to protect the agents. The law made it illegal for states to arrest agents for things that happened while they were doing their job.

The law could keep states from arresting the agents, but it couldn't keep people from shooting at them. Agents discovered that having a marshal with them did not always protect them. Having a posse (group of peacekeepers) with them would not always protect them. Even when there were many agents together, they were in danger.

In Overton County, Tennessee, 11 internal revenue officers discovered this in 1878. They stopped overnight at a farmer's house. Illegal distillers soon surrounded the farmer's home and began attacking. By morning there were almost 200 distillers. The officers managed to slip away and find a log house. The distillers followed. For 42 hours the distillers kept the agents from leaving the house with their guns. Three of the agents were wounded in the attack.

Attacks on revenue agents continued well into the 20th century. Although the work was dangerous, Congress did not end the tax on spirits and tobacco products. The money was too important to the government.

Later, the revenue agents would have even more problems with people who made and sold spirits illegally. But first, they would collect income taxes again.

There have always been Americans who thought income taxes were the best way to raise money for the government. And there have always been people who thought it was an unfair way to raise money. In the 1840s President James Polk said he did not believe it was the purpose of government to provide for the poor. Polk did not think it was right to tax people to raise money to help the poor.

By 1893 many people felt differently. That year there was a major financial depression. That meant the country had a lot of money troubles. There wasn't enough money to go around. Many people were out of work. Now many people wanted the government to help the poor.

In 1894 Congress passed another income tax. It was part of the Wilson Tariff Bill. Many people thought this was a wonderful tax. It only taxed people who made over $4,000 a year. Only 1 in 100 people made this much money. The poor people thought the wealthy people could afford this.

Of course many of the wealthy people did not agree. One man, John Moore, said the law was unconstitutional. That meant the tax law went against the country's most basic law, the Constitution of the United States. The Supreme Court agreed with him. The Constitution said any internal taxes Congress assigned had to be "equally apportioned," that is, they had to be the same everywhere. Congress could not tax only certain people.

Not everyone was happy the income tax was declared unconstitutional. Many Americans wanted a better standard of living. They knew it cost money to run a government. They thought people who made the most money benefited the most from living in America. Therefore, it was thought, those people should pay the most to support the government.

Some powerful politicians supported an income tax as well. President Theodore Roosevelt said in 1907 that "most great civilized countries have an income tax and an inheritance tax. In my judgement both should be part of our system of federal taxation." Soon, support for an income tax was growing, but there was still one problem: the Supreme Court had already found income taxes to be unconstitutional. All Congress and the president could do was debate.

For years Americans and their congressmen talked about income taxes. Finally, they amended the Constitution to say taxes on Americans did not need to tax everyone the same.

In 1909 Congress passed the 16th Amendment to the Constitution. "The Congress shall have power to lay and collect taxes on incomes, from whatever source derived, without apportionment among the several states and without regard to any census or enumeration."

Before it could become part of the Constitution the amendment had to be agreed to by three-fourths of the states. In 1913 Wyoming became the 36th state to agree to the amendment, and it became law. That summer Congress passed an income tax law.

To handle the collection of the new taxes, a Personal Income Tax Division became part of the Bureau of Internal Revenue. Clerks were hired. Tax forms were designed and printed on which people reported their income. Field agents were trained to check taxpayers' figures and send them tax bills. The bureau received so many questions about the new tax that they hired 30 people to do nothing but answer the questions. By the end of 1913 the bureau had 277 employees in the commissioner's office in Washington, D.C., and 3,723 employees elsewhere in the country. Those who did not work in Washington were called the field force.

It took all these people to handle the work, even though only 1 percent of Americans made enough money to pay an income tax. Some 357,598 returns were filed the first year.

Less than a year after the income tax became law, Congress and the president realized that the government would need more money. World War I was starting, so taxes were raised. They were raised again and again as war costs grew. More people had to pay income taxes. There were new taxes on other items: checks, passage tickets, playing cards, admission to entertainments, club dues, telephone messages, telegrams, and insurance. All these taxes had to be collected by the Bureau of Internal Revenue.

By 1915 the new income tax law was already becoming more difficult to understand. One congressman tried to explain why. "I write a law," he said, "you drill a hole in it. I plug the hole. You drill a hole in my plug." People then began using the world "loophole" to mean a legal way to avoid a tax law. These loopholes made the job of collecting taxes even harder. Soon, there were so many people paying taxes for one reason and not another that there weren't enough workers to collect the money. The Bureau of Internal Revenue had to hire more people to keep a careful eye on each new tax the government passed.

By the end of 1917 the number of employees in the Washington office had grown from 277 to 2,243. The bureau established 64 collection districts across the country.

The government's bills for 1917 were almost as much as the total bills for the United States government from 1791 through 1916. The United States government needed a lot more money, and it needed a lot more people to collect it. The Bureau of Internal Revenue continued to grow.

In 1918 the **Prohibition** Act was passed by Congress. This act made it illegal to make or sell alcoholic beverages. As we have seen, taxes on alcoholic beverages had been a large part of the income for the American government almost from the beginning of the nation.

This act had a number of effects on the Bureau of Internal Revenue and the taxes Americans paid. The commissioner of the bureau was put in charge of regulating alcoholic products that were made for legal use.

Now that the government did not have the income from taxes on alcohol, income taxes were increased to make up for that lost money. Revenue employees who had worked to collect taxes on alcoholic beverages were not needed anymore. A lot more employees were needed to work on income taxes.

In 1918 people were also concerned about children working dangerous jobs. Some congressmen thought that they could solve the country's child labor problems while also generating new revenue at the same time. A child labor tax was passed. The tax was 10 percent of the profits of a person or company who employed children. It did not tax all companies that employed children, though. For an employer to be taxed, certain conditions had to be met; the tax could only be applied to companies employing children under 16 who worked in a mine or quarry, children under 14 working in a mill, cannery, workshop, factory, or manufacturing establishment, or on companies that employed children between the ages of 14 and 16 who worked more than eight hours a day or more than six days a week.

At the time this may have seemed like a good law. The country was raising money and probably making more and more employers think twice about using child labor. But in 1922 the Supreme Court declared that the child labor tax law was unconstitutional, and the law was reversed.

In 1919 a special division of the bureau called the Special Intelligence Unit was formed. It investigated people suspected of not paying their taxes and people suspected of helping tax avoiders—including people who worked for the bureau. The men in this unit were sometimes called T-men, short for Treasury Department men.

Some of this unit's most famous cases involved "bootleggers." People did not stop drinking alcohol because of Prohibition. Many people made a lot of money making and selling it illegally. These people were called bootleggers. Many famous and dangerous criminals were involved

T-men, such as Eliot Ness, shown at left, worked for the Treasury Department and helped put "bootleggers" out of business. They often did so by arresting bootleggers for not paying taxes.

in bootlegging. The government wanted to stop this crime. When it failed to prove someone was involved with illegal sales of alcohol, it would try to prove that they did not pay taxes on all of their income. The most famous criminal who was brought to justice in this manner was Al Capone. Capone was the head of a gang of bootleggers in Chicago. He was suspected of ordering many murders, but no one could prove it. The T-men proved he had not paid taxes on his bootlegging income, and the government put him in jail.

This was a dangerous time for the T-men. Many of their lives were threatened, and some of them were killed. In 1934 Congress passed the National Firearms Act. It was meant to keep criminals from purchasing and using machine guns, silencers, and sawed-off shotguns. Special taxes were imposed on people who made, imported, and sold these guns. The Alcohol, Tobacco, and Tax Division was responsible for finding and investigating people who broke this law.

Al Capone was a gangster in Chicago who avoided many attempts to convict him for both murder and breaking Prohibition laws. It was the Bureau of Internal Revenue who finally sent Capone to jail for not paying his taxes.

After World War I, the Great Depression of the 1930s struck America and the rest of the world. People were without jobs for years. Many people lost their homes, their land, everything they owned. Without jobs people couldn't pay taxes. The American government had big money problems.

President Roosevelt came up with a plan called the New Deal. It helped the American people come through the depression. It created jobs, but it cost a lot of money. For that reason, income taxes were increased again. More people had to pay, and the people who had to pay taxes had to pay more taxes than before.

Prohibition was ended in 1933. With alcoholic beverages legal again the government could raise money by taxing them. The bureau had more taxes to collect.

America had barely come out of the depression when the country became involved in World War II. The costs for this war were greater than all the previous wars. Again income taxes were increased. In 1939, 4 million Americans paid income taxes. By the end of the war in 1945, 42.8 million Americans paid income taxes.

In 1950 America became involved in the Korean War. As has happened all through our country's history, war caused a need for more revenue and thus, more taxes. The income tax grew again. So did taxes on items such as gasoline, cars, and of course, liquor and tobacco products. The Bureau of Internal Revenue grew right along with the taxes.

CHAPTER 6

Putting the "Service" in Internal Revenue Service

SIX YEARS AFTER THE end of World War II, America and the Bureau of Internal Revenue had a major shake-up.

In 1951 America learned that some revenue officers were accepting **bribes** from taxpayers. The commissioner of the revenue testified that 50–60 employees were fired each year for taking bribes. Some bribes were paid to keep the officers from collecting more taxes. Some were paid to keep the officers from bringing taxpayers to court.

Congress decided to investigate the bureau. The tax commissioner ordered an examination of all bureau employees' tax returns. Employees also had to complete a questionnaire on their income. Some employees quit rather than fill out the questionnaire.

One of the most disturbing things Congress learned was that some congressmen had asked bureau employees for special favors for their friends. It was common for bureau employees to get their jobs at the request of a congressman. This made it easier for congressmen to influence the employees to do favors for them.

By the time the investigation was over, 167 bureau employees were suspected of crimes involving their jobs and were forced to leave the bureau. People outside the bureau were affected, too. The assistant attorney general of the United States, one of the highest-ranking lawyers in America, was forced to leave his job. A former commissioner of internal revenue went to prison.

The number of people accused and/or convicted sounds high. But almost 200 of the many thousands of bureau employees were accused of crimes. Before the congressional investigation the bureau was already firing people caught accepting bribes.

Even so, Congress decided the bureau should be changed to try to prevent these crimes from happening again. They passed a reorganization plan. Under the plan, appointments by congressmen and other government officials for all but the highest-level jobs would not be allowed. The country was divided into new regions with new regional heads. A new structure for the bureau was established: the national office, below that, regional offices, and below that, district offices. The duties within each area were changed to limit employees' opportunities to commit crimes without being caught.

In July 1953 the name of the bureau was changed from the Bureau of Internal Revenue to the Internal Revenue Service, or IRS for short. This change reminded people that its purpose was to serve the people of the country while collecting taxes.

An Inspection Division also was created. It was responsible for seeing that IRS employees were performing their jobs legally and punishing those who were not.

In 1954 Congress passed the Internal Revenue Code of 1954. It made over 3,000 changes to the tax laws. The

IRS employees had to learn the new laws and make new forms, so taxpayers could properly report their income and deductions under the new laws. They also had to write explanations of the new tax laws for the taxpayers.

In 1955 the IRS was among the first organizations to use computers. The first year, 1.1 million returns were processed using computers. These were only the shortest tax returns, called 1040-As. The use of computers shortened the time it took to check that every tax return was mathematically correct. This meant that the numbers had been added, subtracted, divided, and multiplied correctly.

The IRS employees were not only learning new laws. The employees had never used computers, so they had to learn to how to enter information. Other people were hired who knew what to do about computer problems.

The IRS was among the first government agencies to use computers to help its employees perform their duties. Computers have become more powerful than the ones first used by the IRS, and the agency continues to use new technology.

Convicted mafia boss John Gotti is seen being led to his sentencing hearing. An Organized Crime Drive is required in every IRS district.

Through the years, Congress has passed many new tax laws. Sometimes taxes have gone up, and sometimes they have gone down. Every time a new law is passed, the people in the IRS have to change the tax forms, explain the law in a way people will understand, put the new information into writing, and make it available to taxpayers. The lawyers and accountants who work for the IRS have to keep up with all the changes, so they know what the law is when they check taxpayers' returns. The IRS employees who collect other kinds of internal taxes, like taxes on liquor and tobacco products, have to keep up with changes in those laws, too. The Internal Revenue Service grew and changed as the tax laws grew and changed.

The 1960s were a decade of many changes in the IRS. In 1963 it began helping other countries modernize their tax systems. In 1966 Congress ended the taxes on tobacco products, taxes that had existed for 103 years, though the rates had changed many times during those years. That same year President Lyndon Johnson increased the government's fight against organized crime. An Organized Crime Drive became part of the work in every IRS district.

In 1968 explosives and additional weapons were added to the machine guns and sawed-off shotguns for which the IRS had been responsible since 1934. The Alcohol and Tobacco Tax Division of the IRS was changed to the Alcohol, Tobacco, and Firearms Division. (In 1972 this division was removed from the IRS and became a separate bureau in the Treasury Department.)

Throughout the 1970s the IRS made special efforts to help taxpayers. It started a Volunteer Income Tax Assistance program through which volunteers across the country helped people complete their tax returns for no charge. Toll-free telephone numbers were set up, so people could contact the IRS without paying for the calls. Taxpayer assistance specialists were hired to answer taxpayers' hardest questions. A Problem Resolution program was started to handle taxpayer complaints. The Tax Counseling for the Elderly program was started to help taxpayers past age 59 file their returns.

President Nixon declared a national "War on Drugs" in 1970. As part of this war the IRS investigated tax returns of people suspected of transporting illegal drugs. It hoped to identify unreported income from illegal drug sales.

The IRS also began collecting child support payments from parents who were behind in such payments.

Agents for the Bureau of Alcohol, Tobacco, and Firearms investigate a crime scene. The ATF once fell under the authority of the Internal Revenue Service.

The 1980s were a time of technological changes in the IRS. Tele-Tax service was started, through which taxpayers could call and listen to taped advice on 140 tax topics. The computer system was updated. In 1986 electronic filing of tax returns was used for the first time. That same year 18,000 personal computers were purchased for the IRS. By 1991 the IRS needed 50,000 computer workstations.

The Tax Reform Act of 1986 brought the most changes to the tax laws that the country had seen since the 1950s. That again meant more work for IRS employees preparing new forms and publications to help taxpayers know and follow the new laws.

Because of all the changes throughout the years, the organization was reorganized many times. There were changes in titles, regions, districts, and in the employees' duties. But many people were surprised at the changes that took place in the 1990s.

As the Internal Revenue Service grew, many changes took place in an attempt to make filing taxes easier, but April 15th is always a busy day in post offices as people line up to mail their returns.

7

A New IRS for the New Millennium

IN 1996 SENATOR WILLIAM Roth Jr. was head of the Senate Finance Committee. This is one of two organizations that has the right to conduct an investigation of the IRS. Senator Roth was surprised no Senate Finance Committee had ever conducted a full investigation of the IRS. He decided it was time to do just that.

In September 1997 the committee began hearings. They listened to complaints from taxpayers about the way they had been treated by IRS agents who audited their returns. Complaints from IRS employees who told of cases where they felt taxpayers were not treated fairly by other IRS employees were heard as well. In some of these cases the taxpayers were denied their legal rights.

The committee was dismayed by much of the testimony. They discovered that once again there were people in the IRS who were cheating the taxpayers and the government. The special rights that had been given to IRS employees during the war years and to make it

The Commissioner of the Internal Revenue Service, Charles Rossotti, was brought in to reform America's tax system. One of his main tasks was to make the IRS more helpful to taxpayers.

possible for the IRS to help the government arrest criminals such as bootleggers, murderers and narcotics dealers were being misused. Only a small percentage of the IRS employees were misusing these rights. But these few employees affected thousands of taxpayers.

The committee discovered one of the reasons IRS employees bullied taxpayers was to move ahead in their careers. Promotions were often given based on how much money the collectors had gathered for the government or how many audits resulted in more money for the government. It became more important to the employees to collect money, even if it wasn't owed, than it was to be fair to the taxpayers.

The committee decided things needed to change. It wrote up a plan to reorganize the IRS one more time. Then it sent its plan to the House of Representatives, who passed it and sent it to the Senate. The Senate passed the plan, too. It is called the Internal Revenue Service Reorganization and Reform Act of 1998, known as RRA 98. It called for the largest changes in the IRS since the beginning of the Bureau of Internal Revenue in 1862.

The changes began in July 1998. They are still happening. At the time of this writing many of the changes are still in the planning stage. So what can we expect the IRS to be like in the new century?

The main focus of the restructuring is to shift from collecting taxes at any cost to helping taxpayers meet their obligations to the government.

The main goals of the IRS under RRA 98 are:

★ To understand problems from the taxpayer's point of view;

★ To encourage honesty between IRS employees and taxpayers;

★ To insist on total honesty by IRS employees;

★ To insist managers be accountable. This means if they act in an illegal manner they must be punished for it;

★ And to measure how well an IRS employee does his or her job by how well he/she serves the taxpayers, not by how much money he/she collects for the government.

These new guidelines do not mean the IRS is no longer concerned with collecting taxes. It is very important that the taxes are collected. The government would not be able to run if people could simply decide they would not pay taxes, and there were no agency to make them pay. The purpose of the new rules is to be sure that in the process of collecting the taxes the taxpayers are treated honestly and fairly.

The changes started with a new commissioner of the revenue. The commissioner has always been appointed by the president, and the new commissioner was appointed by President Clinton in 1998. But for the first time the commissioner is not a person who has made a career of working with tax laws. Commissioner Charles Rossotti is a man who started a small computer business in the 1970s and made it into a large, successful company. The president felt that since Rossotti could run a large company, he would know how to manage the IRS, which has over 100,000 employees.

Keeping in mind that the new purpose of the IRS is first to serve the taxpayer, Commissioner Rossotti drew up a plan. It will completely change the way the IRS works.

Before RRA 98, the main office of the IRS was located in Washington, where it will remain. This is where the commissioner has his office, at 1111 Constitution Boulevard. Before RRA 98, the country was broken into four regional offices. Some 33 district offices reported to the regional offices. Branch offices reported to the district offices. The offices were located nearest the taxpayers the offices served.

Below the commissioner and his deputy commissioners, the top people were the regional directors. Beneath them in job importance were deputy directors, chiefs, assistant chiefs, managers, counselors, advocates, auditors, examiners, collectors, and special agents. The IRS was organized in the way it was thought easiest to determine which taxpayers owed how much money, who wasn't paying what they owed, and how to collect what hadn't been paid.

The new plan leaves the commissioner and his deputy commissioner at the top of the IRS organization. The country will no longer be divided into geographical regions. Instead, the organization will be broken into four areas based on the type of taxpayers being served. That way the IRS employees can specialize. They won't have to know all the tax laws, so they can try to help everyone. Instead, they can learn all about the tax laws that affect one type of taxpayer. They will be more knowledgeable and therefore better able to help taxpayers.

The four types of taxpayers are:

★ Wage and investment income taxpayers (W&I);
★ Small business, self-employed, and supplemental income taxpayers, some partnerships and S corporations, and corporations with assets under $5 million (SB/SE/SI);
★ Corporations with more than $5 million in assets (MM/LC);

★ And tax-exempt taxpayers: employee plans, exempt organizations, and state and local governments (TE).

Although the exact plan hasn't been decided upon, it is expected to be something like what follows. The main goals of the IRS centers serving the W&I and SB/SE/SI taxpayers will be:

1. To help taxpayers follow the tax laws by supplying them with the information they need before it is time to file their returns. That is, to see that the proper forms and explanations of the law are available.
2. To answer taxpayers' questions about the tax laws and how to properly report their income and expenses on the tax returns.
3. To make certain that taxpayers are filing correctly. This will be done by checking each return for mathematical errors and checking each return to see that the income and deduction items are statistically normal.

The W&I and SB/SE/SI areas will be responsible for educating taxpayers about the laws. They will keep track of taxpayer accounts, that is, how much tax has been withheld or paid for each year.

The large corporate area, or MM/LC, might be organized by similar industries: for instance, financial services and health care, food and retail, technology and media, energy and chemicals, and heavy manufacturing and transportation.

The tax-exempt area will likely be separated by the three major types of tax-exempt customers: employee plans, exempt organizations, and governmental agencies. An important part of the work with employee plan and exempt organization taxpayers will be to see that they know what is necessary to be a tax-exempt organization and keep the laws governing tax-exempt organizations. Governmental agencies, states and cities, often issue bonds to raise money. The

IRS employees serving this group will make certain the bonds meet the requirements of tax-exempt bonds.

There will be service centers for each of the four taxpayer areas. The service centers will process the returns. A lot goes into processing a return. Every one that is filed is checked for mathematical accuracy.

People receive many different forms each year telling how much money different organizations pay them. Employers send W-2s telling how much money they paid the person, how much federal and state tax and Social Security and Medicare tax was withheld, and numerous other items regarding the person's employment. Banks send 1099-INT forms to tell how much interest they paid the taxpayer during the year. They send 1098-INT forms to tell how much money the taxpayer paid the bank for interest on house loans. Investment companies send 1099-DIVs and 1099-Bs to tell how much money the taxpayer earned in dividends and how much money the taxpayer made from selling investments.

The IRS service center compares all the 1099s and W-2s sent to a taxpayer to the amounts the taxpayer reported on his tax return. This is usually done by comparing the Social Security number on the W-2s and 1099s to the Social Security number on the taxpayer's tax return.

Under the new IRS there will be a national taxpayer advocate, or NTA for short. "Advocate" means "one who pleads the cause of another." The National Taxpayer Advocate is a person who goes to others in the IRS to present taxpayers' problems.

The NTA's responsibilities are to:

★ Help taxpayers find solutions for problems with the IRS;

★ Identify areas where taxpayers have trouble dealing with the IRS;

★ Suggest changes in IRS practices and tax laws to make it easier for taxpayers to deal with the IRS;

★ Supervise local taxpayer advocate offices (there will be at least one office in each state);

★ Issue Taxpayer Assistance Orders when taxpayers may be in trouble with the IRS. These orders will include information on the help available throughout the NTA and how to contact the state and national taxpayer advocates;

★ Prepare reports twice a year for Congress. These reports have two purposes: (1) to point out tax laws that are hard for taxpayers and the IRS to follow and suggest solutions; and (2) point out the most common reasons for lawsuits between the IRS and taxpayers and suggest ways to decrease them.

The information the Taxpayer Advocates receive from taxpayers will not be shared with other IRS departments.

The RRA 98 established an Oversight Board to oversee the IRS. The board will have nine members: the commissioner of the revenue, the secretary of the treasury, one federal employee, and six people who do not work for the federal government.

The board is to ensure taxpayers are being treated respectfully and fairly by the IRS. It is to review the plans for changes and goals for the IRS. It will decide whether high-ranking IRS officers are doing their jobs and whether they should be kept on or fired.

Does all this attention to taxpayers' rights mean the IRS will no longer be concerned about whether taxpayers are paying as much in taxes as the law says they are to pay? No.

There will still be collectors. There will still be audits of taxpayers. There will still be criminal investigations. The IRS will still be on the lookout for taxpayers who do not report all of their income or who report deductions that were not real. But now there are laws in place to make it tougher for a few dishonest IRS employees to treat taxpayers unfairly.

The changes under the RRA 98 will take years to put into place. As we have seen, the IRS has been constantly

In 1996 the Montana Freemen, seen here meeting with a negotiator, refused to pay federal taxes, and an armed standoff with federal law enforcement agents ended in their arrest after 53 days.

changing from the time it began. It grows and decreases in size depending upon the tax laws of the times and the needs of the American people. No doubt it will continue to grow and change even after all the planned changes from RRA 98 have taken place.

Tax laws will continue to change, too. Tax rates will increase and decrease, then increase and decrease again. Income tax rates and laws will change. Tax rates and laws on other items such as alcohol, tobacco, and guns will change.

One thing will not change. The government will always need money. No one has found a way yet for government to survive without some kind of taxes. As long as our government needs taxes to raise money, we will have a revenue organization to collect the money. As a reminder of the necessity of taxes, former Supreme Court Justice Oliver Wendell Holmes's comment on taxes appears over the door of the IRS building in Washington, D.C.: "Taxes are what we pay for a civilized society."

Glossary

Bribe—Money or a favor given to someone in a position of power or trust.

Customs—Taxes on imports or exports. See *tariff.*

Debt—Money owed to another.

Direct tax—A tax paid by the people to the government.

Duty—Tax on imports.

Export—Items made in one state or country and sent to another to be sold.

External tax—Tax on things sent out of the country or brought into the country to be sold.

Import—Items brought into a country from another country to be sold.

Indirect tax—A tax that is not paid on income, but on things a person chooses to buy; examples: sales tax, property tax.

Internal tax—Tax on items which are made and sold in the same state or country.

Prohibition—A law making it illegal to make or sell alcoholic drinks.

Revenue—Money a government collects.

Revenue agent—A person who helps collect or record taxes.

Stamp tax—A tax that requires a stamp to be placed on items to show the tax on those items has been paid.

Tariff—Tax on imports or exports. See *customs.*

Taxes—Money paid to a government.

Tax rebellion—A protest by citizens against taxes (also called a tax revolt).

Further Reading

Hakim, Joy. *From Colonies to Country.* NY: Oxford University Press Children's Books, 1999.

Marshall, Peter, and David, Manuel. *From Sea to Shining Sea for Children: Discovering God's Plan for America in Her First Half-Century of Independence 1787–1837.* Grand Rapids, Michigan: Fleming H. Revell, 1993.

Nardo, Don. ed. *The Declaration of Independence: A Model for Individual Rights.* San Diego: Lucent, 1999.

Sobel, Syl. *How the United States Government Works.* NY: Barron's Educational Series, Inc., 1999.

Smith, Barbara C. *After the Revolution: The Smithsonian History of Everyday Life in the Eighteenth Century.* NY: Pantheon, 1985.

Smith, Carter, ed. *Governing and Teaching: A Sourcebook on Colonial America.* Brookfield, CT: The Millbrook Press, 1991.

Treasury's Page for Kids. www.ustreas.gov/kids (The U.S. Dept. of the Treasury explains how the government makes, regulates, and collects money.)

Index

ABOUT THE AUTHOR: JoAnn A. Grote loves to read and write about history. She has written over 20 historical novels for adults and children. Her short stories and articles have been published in magazines including *'Teen* and *Guideposts for Kids*. JoAnn worked at the historical restoration of Old Salem in Winston-Salem, North Carolina, for five years. Today she lives in Minnesota.

SENIOR CONSULTING EDITOR Arthur M. Schlesinger, jr. is the leading American historian of our time. He won the Pulitzer Prize for his book *The Age of Jackson* (1945) and again for *A Thousand Days* (1965). This chronicle of the Kennedy Administration also won a National Book Award. Professor Schlesinger is the Albert Schweitzer Professor of the Humanities at the City University of New York, and he has been involved in several other Chelsea House projects, including the REVOLUTIONARY WAR LEADERS and COLONIAL LEADERS series.

Picture Credits